DISCARD

# HOW PLANTS GROW

CATHLEEN SMALL

Britannica®
Educational Publishing

IN ASSOCIATION WITH

ROSEN
EDUCATIONAL SERVICES

Published in 2019 by Britannica Educational Publishing (a trademark of Encyclopædia Britannica, Inc.) in association with The Rosen Publishing Group, Inc.
29 East 21st Street, New York, NY 10010

Distributed exclusively by Rosen Publishing.
To see additional Britannica Educational Publishing titles, go to rosenpublishing.com.

First Edition

**Britannica Educational Publishing**
J.E. Luebering: Executive Director, Core Editorial
Mary Rose McCudden: Editor, Britannica Student Encyclopedia

**Rosen Publishing**
Louise Eaton: Editor
Nelson Sá: Art Director
Nicole Russo-Duca: Designer & Book Layout
Cindy Reiman: Photography Manager

**Library of Congress Cataloging-in-Publication Data**

Names: Small, Cathleen, author.
Title: How plants grow / Cathleen Small.
Description: New York : Britannica Educational Publishing, in Association with Rosen Educational Services, 2019. | Series: Let's find out! plants | Audience: Grades 1–4. | Includes bibliographical references and index.
Identifiers: LCCN 2017044423 | ISBN 9781538301890 (library bound) | ISBN 9781538301906 (pbk.) | ISBN 9781538301913 (6 pack)
Subjects: LCSH: Growth (Plants—Juvenile literature. | Plants—Development—Juvenile literature.
Classification: LCC QK731 .S58 2019 | DDC 575.9/7—dc23
LC record available at https://lccn.loc.gov/2017044423

*Manufactured in the United States of America*

**Photo credits**: Cover, interior pages background image AustralianCamera/Shutterstock.com; p. 4 Stockbyte/Thinkstock; p. 5 © Corbis; p. 6 sichkarenko.com/Shutterstock.com; p. 7 PHB.cz/Fotolia; pp. 8, 9, 13, 14, 17 © Encyclopedia Britannica, Inc.; p. 10 © Herbert Esser/Fotolia; p. 11 © Stephen J. Krasemann/The National Audubon Society Collection/Photo Researchers; p. 12 beppenob/Fotolia; p. 15 nook kie/ Shutterstock.com; p. 16 © MedioImages/Getty Images; p. 18 © Robert J. Ashworth/The National Audubon Society Collection/Photo Researchers; p. 19 BGSmith/Shutterstock.com; p. 20 luchschen_shutter/Fotolia; p. 21 Simon Kadula/Shutterstock.com; p. 22 Xico Putini/Fotolia; p. 23 Scott Bauer/ARS/USDA; p. 24 ehrlif/Fotolia; p. 25 John Anderson/Fotolia; p. 26 © V. Zhuravlev/Fotolia; p. 27 Sergey Mostovoy/Fotolia; p. 28 OhEngine/Shutterstock.com; p. 29 © Nigel Cattlin/Holt Studios International/Photo Researchers, Inc.

# CONTENTS

Plants                          4

Life Cycle of Plants            6

Germination                     8

Sprouting                       10

Blooming                        12

Pollination                     14

Dissemination                   16

Competition                     20

Plant Disease                   22

Pollution                       26

Death                           28

Glossary                        30

For More Information            31

Index                           32

# Plants

Plants are organisms that exist in most places on Earth. Hundreds of thousands of different species, or kinds, of plant grow on Earth. Some plants are so tiny that people can hardly see them. Some are grasses that spread over large areas. Others are trees that grow as tall as very tall buildings. Some are mosses that may live on other plants.

Most plants have several things in common. They are not able to move around. Their cells

**Mosses are tiny plants that grow on moist ground, rocks, or trees.**

have stiff walls made of a tough material called cellulose. They also grow.

Plants grow nearly everywhere on Earth. Most plants grow in soil, but some plants do not need soil. Plants called epiphytes can grow on other plants or on objects without getting nutrients from them.

Plants need sunshine, water, and air to grow. All green plants use the sun's energy, water, and a gas called carbon dioxide to make their food. This process is called photosynthesis.

Bamboo is actually a type of tall grass that can look like a tree.

# LIFE CYCLE OF PLANTS

A life cycle is a series of changes that happens to all living things as they grow and age. The cycle begins with a seed, a spore, or special kinds of stems that can grow into another plant. With the proper nutrients, water, and sunshine, the plant grows to become an adult.

The adult plant may form flowers or another reproductive organ. Then the plant produces new seeds or spores. When wind, water, birds, insects, or other animals

Pinecones contain the reproductive structures for plants called conifers.

The flowering of plants like daffodils, tulips, and hyacinths is part of their life cycle.

disperse those, the life cycle can begin again in a new plant. All plants go through similar processes in their life cycles, but in this book, only plants that produce seeds will be described.

## THINK ABOUT IT

Plants native to the East Coast of the United States have been found growing on the West Coast. How did those plants get so far from their original homes?

7

# GERMINATION

Once a seed has formed, it leaves its parent plant. A seed will **germinate** once it is in the ground and water, soil, and temperature conditions are right.

Seeds often can stay dormant, or inactive, for many years before they germinate. Because of this, people can store seeds and plant them later. Plants that do not produce seeds have less time before their offspring

During germination, the seed coat breaks open to allow part of the embryo to emerge.

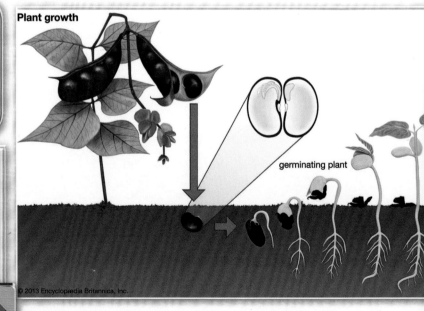

Plant growth

germinating plant

© 2013 Encyclopædia Britannica, Inc.

Corn kernel

whole — cross section

seed coat

endosperm

embryo

© 2013 Encyclopædia Britannica, Inc.

must germinate. Sometimes the plant's offspring does not leave the parent before beginning to grow.

A seed contains a miniature plant called an embryo. It can develop into a fully grown plant. The outer shell of a seed, called a seed coat, protects the embryo. Inside the seed

**The embryo is contained within a seed coat and endosperm, a type of tissue that feeds the embryo.**

a nutritious material provides food for the embryo. In flowering plants this material is called endosperm. When the seed germinates, the embryo begins to change. As germination begins, parts of the embryo break out of the seed coat.

# SPROUTING

One part of germination is sprouting. Sprouting is a stage of growth. It is the step that occurs after the embryo breaks out of the seed coat. Sprouting occurs before a plant becomes an adult.

When sprouting happens, one part of an embryo grows downward. It becomes the plant's roots and takes in water and food from the soil. Other parts grow upward. They become the plant's stem and leaves. Stems and leaves absorb sunlight and air. Seeds need a certain amount of

A great many plants sprout in early spring, after soaking up water and nutrients from rain and snow during the winter.

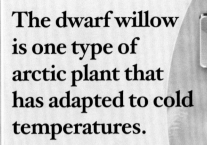

The dwarf willow is one type of arctic plant that has adapted to cold temperatures.

water to sprout but not too much. Too much water can kill the seed. Seeds also need the right temperature to develop. Some seeds germinate and sprout in cold temperatures. Others need warm temperatures.

## COMPARE AND CONTRAST

Why do roots move toward the ground while stems and leaves move upward?

# Blooming

Flowers bloom on some plants when the plant becomes an adult. A flower is the part of a plant that makes a seed. Flowers vary widely in their shape, size, color, and scent. Many types are small and barely noticeable. The blossoms that most people think of as flowers are those that are colorful and showy. Usually, a flower is easy to tell apart from its stem or roots.

The main seed-making parts of a flower are the stamen, pistil, and ovary. The shape of a flower is meant

Not all flowers are bright and showy, but peony blossoms are.

to protect these parts. Other parts are called the calyx and the corolla. They work together to protect the pistil and stamen so that the life cycle can continue.

In this diagram, both pistil and stamens are shown.

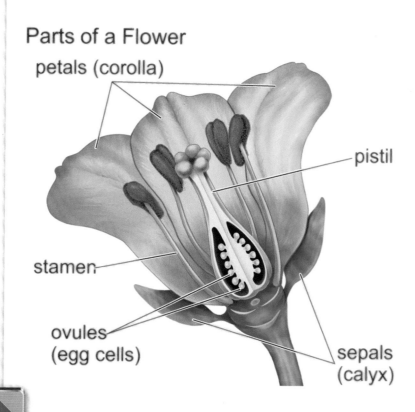

**Parts of a Flower**

petals (corolla)

pistil

stamen

ovules (egg cells)

sepals (calyx)

# POLLINATION

Pollination is the process by which flowers form seeds. This is how plants reproduce.

There are two main kinds of pollination: self-pollination and cross-pollination. Self-pollination is the transfer of pollen from a stamen to a pistil on the same plant. This can happen within one flower

Bees can help some plants cross-pollinate.

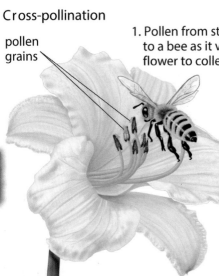
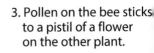

Cross-pollination

pollen grains

1. Pollen from stamens sticks to a bee as it visits a flower to collect food.

3. Pollen on the bee sticks to a pistil of a flower on the other plant.

pollen

2. The bee travels to another plant of the same type.

or between different flowers on the same plant. Cross-pollination is the transfer of pollen from a flower on one plant to a flower on another plant.

Flowers depend on carriers for cross-pollination. Carriers are things that carry pollen from one plant to another. They include the wind as well as insects, birds, and other animals.

After a grain of pollen lands on a flower's pistil, fertilization occurs. That is, a sperm cell from the pollen enters the egg cell in the pistil. The fertilized egg then grows into a seed.

# DISSEMINATION

Seeds have to spread to a place where they can grow. They can be spread by many methods. One of these is gravity. Sometimes the seed is contained in a fruit, like a tomato. When the fruit falls and breaks open, the seed can germinate in the soil where it lands. Some seeds are not contained a fruit. They are produced on a cone, which can also fall to the ground.

Other times, the wind carries seeds away from their parent plant. Sunflower seeds, for example, live in sunflower plants that can grow

Sunflower plants have hundreds of tiny seeds that are spread by wind.

## How Seeds Travel

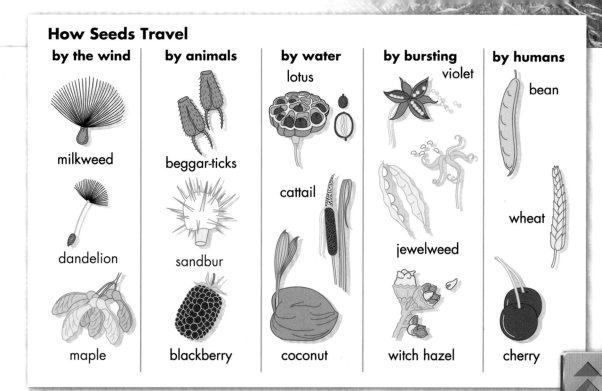

| by the wind | by animals | by water | by bursting | by humans |
|---|---|---|---|---|
| milkweed | beggar-ticks | lotus | violet | bean |
| dandelion | sandbur | cattail | jewelweed | wheat |
| maple | blackberry | coconut | witch hazel | cherry |

**THINK ABOUT IT**

What features do you think you might find in seeds that are spread by gravity compared to seeds that are spread by the wind?

Seeds can spread in many ways. They can be carried by forces, or they can just fall to the ground.

several feet tall. When the plant is mature, the wind can blow the seeds away from the parent plant into a new location.

Cattails are wetland plants that disseminate their seeds by wind.

Some plants, such as peas, expel their seeds with force. When a pea pod, which holds the seeds, dries and shrinks, it pulls apart with a twisting motion that pops the peas loose and expels them from the plant.

Water can carry seeds, too. Coconut seeds have a **husk** that allows the fruit to float. Because coconuts often grow near oceans, it is not unusual for coconut seeds to float hundreds

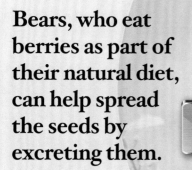

Bears, who eat berries as part of their natural diet, can help spread the seeds by excreting them.

of miles in the water before landing in another place and germinating.

Animals sometimes spread seeds, too. For example, berries contain many seeds. Animals like deer, bears, and others eat the berries. When they later excrete the seeds as waste, the seeds can germinate where the animal excreted them. Sometimes seeds get attached to the fur of animals, too, and drop off in new locations.

# COMPETITION

If too many plants try to grow in a small area, they may not grow at all. If they do grow, they may have trouble fully developing. These plants are competing, or struggling to access the same resources.

A resource is a place or thing that provides something useful. Competing for resources is one of the most basic interactions in life. Living things may compete for several resources

**Farmers carefully plant corn to ensure that the plants are not overcrowded.**

## THINK ABOUT IT

Farmers plant crops in fields. Sometimes the plants can spread and reproduce in places that a farmer might not have intended. What can farmers do to control this?

at once. However, one resource is usually the most critical for survival.

Over time, competition can change a community. When a plant in an area is no longer able to get the resources it needs, all of its kind can die out.

Weeds prevent useful plants from getting the resources they need to thrive.

# PLANT DISEASE

Plants can get diseases, or illnesses, just as animals do. People worry mainly about the diseases that affect crop plants, which are the plants that farmers grow for humans and other animals to eat. Crop diseases often cause great losses of food and money.

Plant diseases may be divided into two groups: infectious diseases and noninfectious diseases. Some botanists, or scientists who study plants, find ways to treat plant diseases. Infectious diseases can spread from one

**Blight is one example of a plant disease that can be devastating.**

plant to another. These diseases are caused by particles called viruses and tiny living things like fungi and bacteria. Plants that live on or inside other plants may also cause disease.

Most plant diseases are caused by fungi, such as rusts, smuts, and mildews. Fungi that get their food from living plants and animals are called parasites.

Blight on Ireland's potato crops led to many deaths during the nineteenth-century potato famine.

Few native plants grow well in sand, which is why many beaches have little plant life growing on them.

Noninfectious diseases cannot be spread from one plant to another. However, these diseases are a major cause of poor health in plants. They are often caused by conditions in the environment.

If there are not enough minerals in the soil, plant growth can slow down. That makes the plant weak, and it does not grow properly.

Some plants grow well in wet areas. However, too much water can be a problem for many plants.

Too much water can also be a problem for plants. Extra water lowers the amount of oxygen in the soil, which causes poor root growth. Extra water may cause plants to have a weak cell wall that allows other diseases in. Plants may also become diseased when the acid level of the soil is too high or too low.

**COMPARE AND CONTRAST**

Explain which you think would be harder for a farmer to control: infectious disease or noninfectious disease.

# POLLUTION

Plants need a healthy environment to survive. Pollution, which means things like waste, chemicals, or other harmful substances, threatens the environment. Pollution affects the air, the water, and the land.

Air pollution leads to acid rain, or polluted rain. Acid rain can harm living things. It causes crop plants and forest trees to become diseased and, in some cases, to die. In addition, air pollution may cause Earth's average temperature to rise. Plants depend on uncontaminated rainwater and a predictable temperature. Air pollution can therefore be very disruptive to the life cycle of plants.

Pollutants from activities like coal burning can contribute to acid rain.

Water pollution can have a devastating impact on the plants that depend on that water source.

**THINK ABOUT IT**

What do you think you can do to try to limit the pollution in your area?

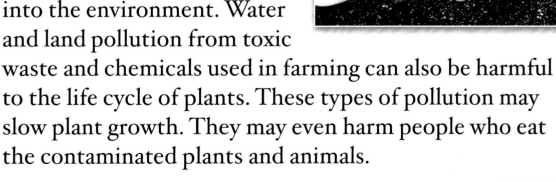

The water and land can be polluted by things like the garbage that people dump and by the poisonous waste that some companies release into the environment. Water and land pollution from toxic waste and chemicals used in farming can also be harmful to the life cycle of plants. These types of pollution may slow plant growth. They may even harm people who eat the contaminated plants and animals.

# DEATH

The last step of a plant's life cycle is death. A plant, like every other living thing, will eventually die. Plants can die of old age, from disease, or from the destruction of their bodies.

One reason plants die is because they receive too much or too little of the resources they need. If plants do not get enough water or sunlight, they cannot absorb nutrients or minerals, and they will not grow. If they get too much water, it causes the roots to suffocate. Finally, if they get too much sunlight, they will wilt.

**Too much sunlight or not enough water can cause plants to wilt and die.**

Plants also need the correct temperature and amount of soil to grow. Soil naturally loses nutrients over time, so sometimes nutrients need to be added to soil to make sure that plants do not die.

If a plant reproduces, its children will live on. This is how a species keeps from going extinct.

Plants can rot if the water, temperature, and nutrients they get are out of balance.

29

# GLOSSARY

**bacteria** Tiny living things that can cause diseases.

**disperse** To spread around.

**endosperm** A food-containing tissue formed within the seed in seed plants.

**epiphyte** A plant that gets moisture and the materials needed to make its food from the air and rain.

**expel** To drive or force out.

**extinct** No longer existing.

**fertilize** To make (an egg) able to grow and develop.

**gravity** The force that makes things fall to Earth, such as when they are dropped.

**infectious** Capable of causing infection.

**mature** Fully grown or developed.

**native** Naturally occurring in a certain place.

**noninfectious** Not capable of causing infection.

**nutrient** Something that a plant or animal needs in order to function and grow.

**pistil** The seed-producing part of a flower.

**pollination** The transfer of pollen onto the part of the flower that makes seeds.

**pollution** Substances that harm the environment.

**reproductive** Of, relating to, or capable of creating a new organism from its parents.

**sperm** The male reproductive cell.

**spore** A reproductive body that consists of a single cell and can develop into a new individual.

**stamen** An organ of a flower that produces pollen.

# FOR MORE INFORMATION

## Books

Dickmann, Nancy. *Plant Structures*. New York, NY: Cavendish Square, 2016.

Platt, Richard. *Plants Bite Back*. London, UK: DK Children, 2013.

Rattini, Kristin Baird. *National Geographic Readers: Seed to Plant*. Washington, DC: National Geographic Children's Books, 2014.

Richardson, Gillian. *10 Plants That Shook the World*. Toronto, ON: Annick Press, 2013.

Slingerland, Janet. *The Secret Lives of Plants!* North Mankato, MN: Capstone Press, 2014.

Terrazas, April Chloe. *Botany: Plants, Cells and Photosynthesis*. Austin, TX: Crazy Brainz, 2014.

## Websites

**Gardening Know How**
https://www.gardeningknowhow.com/special/children/how-plants-grow.htm
Twitter: @GardenKnowHow; Facebook, Instagram: @GardeningKnowHow

**Kidport**
http://www.kidport.com/RefLib/Science/HowPlantsGrow/HowPlantsGrow.htm
Twitter, Facebook: @kidport

**Wonderopolis**
https://wonderopolis.org/wonder/how-do-seeds-sprout
Twitter, Facebook, Instagram: @wonderopolis

# INDEX

animals, as pollen and seed carriers, 15, 19

blooming, 12–13

calyx, 13
carbon dioxide, 5
cellulose, 5
chlorophyll, 23
coconuts, 18
competition, 20–21
corolla, 13
crop plants, 21, 22, 26
cross-pollination, 14, 15

death, 28–29
distribution, 7, 16–19

egg cell, 15
embryo, 9, 10
endosperm, 9
epiphytes, 5

fertilization, 15
flowers, 6, 9, 12, 14, 15, 16

force, 18
fungi, 23

germination, 8–9, 16, 19
gravity, 16, 17

husks, 18

infectious diseases, 22–23, 25

leaves, 8, 10, 11, 23

mosses, 4

noninfectious diseases, 22, 24
nutrients, 5, 6, 28, 29

organisms, 4
ovary, 12

peas, 18
photosynthesis, 5
pistil, 12, 13, 14, 15

plants, characteristics of, 4–5
pollination, 14–15
pollution, 26–27

resources, 20–21, 28
roots, 10, 11, 23, 25, 28

seed coat, 9, 10
seeds, 6, 7, 8, 9, 10, 11, 12, 14, 15, 16–19
self-pollination, 14–15
sperm cell, 15
sprouting, 10–11
stamen, 12, 13, 14
stem, 6, 10, 11, 12, 23
sun, 5, 6, 10, 28
sunflowers, 16–17

temperature, 8, 11, 26, 29
trees, 4, 26

water, 5, 6, 8, 10, 11, 18, 19, 25, 26, 27, 28
wind, 6, 15, 16, 17